12 Days to the Rescue!
A Colorful Christmas

By Christine Berg

Truly Unique Gifting

Welcome to Christmas gifting made fun! This book gives you all the assistance you need to put together unforgettable presents for everyone in your life. Whether you would like to provide group presents for multiple families or give a single person a special gift, this guide takes away all the guesswork and leaves you giving a truly distinctive gift that will be loved by all!

Other Books in this Series:

Trim the Tree at Christmas

Christmas Around the World

A Partridge in a Pear Tree Christmas

Caroling Through Christmas

www.12daystotherescue.com

Cover design by Ember & Co Design Studio

12 Days to the Rescue
A Colorful Christmas

Christine Berg
Cover design by Ember & Co Design Studio

ISBN: 978-1-7328150-2-5

To Ethan & Chelsea

A perfect pairing

My favorite power couple

INTRODUCTION

I am not a good gifter. I try, I really do, but that clever, thoughtful, just-right something that will be loved and cherished forever (or thoroughly enjoyed in the moment) usually escapes me. I did it once: the year I got my Dad a leather tool-belt. He didn't ask for it, but I could tell when he opened the present that it completely hit the mark and he really loved it. So, I know the feeling- that wonderful satisfaction of pleasing your givee. But because that rarely happened, Christmas shopping for me was agony. I am not overstating. Even after my budget allowed a wider range of choices, finding that elusive "perfect gift" for siblings, grandparents, parents and in-laws was pressure filled and painful. If you can relate, then *12 Days to the Rescue* is for you! It will literally rescue you from suffering and distress. (OK- maybe a little overstating). This book follows a theme of gifts for 12 days starting with Christmas that can be customized for everyone on your shopping list. There are options given for different ages, individuals, families and monetary amounts. I give you the tags and ideas for wrapping. You can do as much or little as you like with this. People <u>love</u> these! So, with the stressful question of, "What do I get them?" taken care of, you can relax knowing you are giving a great gift and actually enjoy the rest of the holiday season. You will become an awesome gifter and finally it truly will be better to give than to receive.

Twelve days of gifts?! That might seem a lot harder and costlier than one nice gift per person. If you can do that- find what you want on the web, click a few times and have your gift magically sent off to give Christmas spirit- go for it! I highly recommend it. However, if scrolling through hundreds of items online or scouring aisles in stores to find what you want, or even to know what you want, leaves you glassy-eyed and feeling frustrated, this book is a real de-stressor. This works especially well when gifting many families. And, when you buy in bulk to split apart, it really does get less expensive. Now let's get started!

Tips:
- ❖ First things first: Establish a budget- either per person or per household. Divide by 12 for your allotted amount per gift day. Obviously if you spend less on one day, you can allocate that to spend a little more an another.
- ❖ The earlier in the year you begin, the more you can watch for sales!
- ❖ Buy in bulk and split up whenever possible.
- ❖ If you are a baker, gifts of mixes or baked treats are great fun and stretch easily for several recipients.
- ❖ Often one gift can serve a whole family.
- ❖ When ordering items online, give yourself time for things to be delivered to you before you need to send them on. If you are mailing your 12 Days to the Rescue gifts, remember the post office deadlines.
- ❖ Collecting fun things to give away does take up space; you may want to dedicate a couple of shelves in a closet to keep everything sorted and stored.
- ❖ *Please personalize this as much as possible!* I am only giving suggestions, you know the tastes of those you are gifting the best!

A Colorful Christmas!

Have fun sharing holidays with the classic- and also unusual colors- of Christmas. Our gifting theme celebrates Christmas with twelve days of color. Each day's gift will be centered around a different hue.

Any gift that is the color of the day would be perfect. I give suggestions to spark ideas. Gift tags are provided for your use at the end of the book. The pictures offer enhancement suggestions for the crafty among you. Have fun with it!

Wrapping recommendation: Wrap each day's gift in it's corresponding color. That can be solid, patterned, bold, or soft. Check out the pictures for ideas and inspiration.

MERRY CHRISTMAS!

The very first thing your giftees will receive is a card that carries the explanation of what you are giving this year. You need only one per giving group. (i.e. only one for your sister, her husband and kids, but also one for your grandfather, who lives alone). This truly piques excitement! Opening a present starts on Christmas Day, so if your tradition is celebrating Christmas Eve, on that night they open the card only. If you celebrate on Christmas Day, they would open the card along with the first day's gift. On the gift tag, write a personal note for that special touch!

The First Day of Christmas: December 25th

We are starting our colorful celebration with the color ORANGE. What is orange during the holiday season? I love the picture of family and friends gathered around a crackling fire with expectant stockings hung above.

Gift Ideas: (mix & match, pick & choose)

- For **Couples** or whole **Families**: If there are campers among them, give campfire gifts. S'mores treats or a kit would be a fun gift.
- For **Adults**: Going along with the fire theme, give seasonally scented candles with an unusual box of matches. For those that cook with fire, anything for their BBQ. If they have a fireplace in their home, give fireplace accessories- fire starters, a scented log or decorative log-holders. Fiery hot sauce is a fun, play-on-words gift.
- For **Teens**: Responsible teens would love food-scented candles. Along with s'mores, there are different campfire food treats that would make a great kit. Look online for fun recipes. Or give a new stocking for them to hang.
- For **Kids**: New stockings can turn into keepsakes. Or give anything camping (even if it's just in their backyard); don't forget the fun desserts!

The Second Day of Christmas: December 26th

Today's color is RED. This classic traditional color can be seen everywhere this time of year. Anything red is Christmassy!

Gift Ideas: (mix & match, pick & choose)
- For **Everyone**: Anything that is red. Suggestions: ornaments, candy, clothing items (sweaters, socks, scarves), recreational items (playground balls), home décor (seasonal pillows, throws, holiday dishes), jewelry. If its red, it works!

The Third Day of Christmas: December 27th

YELLOW is the color of the day. The Bethlehem Star that the wise men followed comes to mind! Center this gift on the stars.

Gift Ideas: (mix & match, pick & choose)

- For **Couples, Adults** or **Families**: Yellow-frosted star-shaped sugar cookies would please a crowd! You can give a blanket, thermos and hot cocoa mix and encourage star gazing. A young couple might appreciate a nice new star for the top of their tree. A telescope would be an interesting gift also. Galaxy related books or movies would apply.
- For **Teens**: Travel mugs with the star-gazing encouragement would be a great gift here. Add on a gift certificate to their favorite coffee shop. A telescope might just spark a new hobby.
- For **Kids**: Give glow-in-the-dark star stickers for their room. Or a night-light that projects stars onto the ceiling.

The Fourth Day of Christmas: December 28th

Today's color is another classic, GREEN! We see this color especially in wreaths, in decorating and, of course, the Christmas tree. To be green is also to be environmentally responsible. If you go that route, be sure to mention it in your gift tag.

Gift Ideas: (mix & match, pick & choose)

- For **Families**: They might enjoy a terrarium kit that they all work together to complete. For the ambitious, you can give each member their own fir tree sapling. Or you can give each person a particularly meaningful ornament to hang on their tree.
- For **Couples & Adults**: Give a wreath, swag or other décor made of greens. A live Christmas Cactus is a great gift. Be environmentally aware and give a "green" gift- anything that is a sustainable product.
- **Teens**: Young people today would really appreciate a gift that is ecologically responsible- one that is sustainable or made from recycled materials. Anything reusable, recycled or repurposed is a good choice. Seedlings or an herb garden kit might be a good option.
- **Kids**: You can give a Christmas tree sapling that they will have for years to come. Or look up "recycled toys" or "green toys" to give a sustainable, green gift.

The Fifth Day of Christmas: December 29th

Today's color is PINK. Certainly not a traditional holiday color. What is pink? Why the Sugar Plum Fairy from the Nutcracker story! This day's gift will be in honor of her.

Gift Ideas: (mix & match, pick & choose)

- For **Families:** A working nutcracker and a bag of holiday nuts would be a great gift. And/or you can give something tasty that is full of sugar- candy or fudge! Plum jelly would also work with this theme.
- For **Couples & Adults:** There is a decorative nutcracker to fit every personal style from traditional to modern. Have fun finding just the right one to match your givee. The real nutcracker and bag of nuts is also a festive treat.
- For **Teens:** A personal nutcracker is a very nice gift. So is the sugary one!
- For **Kids**: There are many children's books and videos of the Nutcracker. This could become a favorite Christmas tradition for years to come.

12 Days to the Rescue

The Sixth Day of Christmas: December 30th

Today's color is GOLD. At this time of year, we think of friends, both new and old. Remember the song phrase, "One is silver and the other gold?" We will remember our gold friends today.

Gift Ideas: (mix & match, pick & choose)
- For **Everyone**: Book stores and specialty shops carry very complex and beautiful Christmas cards. Give one per person or per family unit for them to give to a dear gold friend this Christmas.
- For **Everyone**: Some people's best friends are actually their pets. If this is the case a gift card to the local pet shop would be perfect.
- For **Couples** & **Adults**: You can give lotto tickets and hope they "strike gold!" (Check minimum age requirements).
- For **Teens & Kids**: Anything that has a gold touch to it works here. Chocolate gold coins are a fun choice.

The Seventh Day of Christmas: December 31st
New Year's Eve!

As the clock strikes midnight, the sky is BLACK- which is the color of seventh day of Christmas. Give a gift that celebrates the turning of the year.

Gift Ideas: (mix & match, pick & choose)
- For **Families**: Give a New Year's Eve party! Send a hat and a noise maker for each person. You can add some midnight snacks.
- For **Couples** and **Adults**: Give their favorite drink to toast in the New Year. And/or send along those midnight snacks.
- For **Teens**: Fun, special snacks to share with friends this night would be perfect.
- For **Kids**: Give them noise-makers and dress-up hats for a New Year's Eve celebration. They can have fun with those for months to come.

The Eighth Day of Christmas: January 1st
New Year's Day!

Today's color is BLUE. A blue winter sky is particularly beautiful in the morning. On this first morning of the new year, enjoy some "blue" inspired morning treats.

Gift Ideas: (mix & match, pick & choose)

- For **Everyone:** Think blueberries. Give blueberry pancake mixes, or bake blueberry muffins. You can send blueberry jams and jellies. You can give gift cards to a favorite breakfast restaurant. Chocolate covered blueberries can be an added treat.

The Ninth Day of Christmas: January 2nd

WHITE is for…snow! This day's gift will center around the cold fluffy stuff.

Gift Ideas: (mix & match, pick & choose)
- For **Families:** Those that live in warm climates might appreciate a beautiful winter scene puzzle to enjoy together. A snow globe kit is a great family activity. The movie, Frozen ® would be fun for everyone. A gift card to a local snow-cone or ice-cream place would be perfect.
- For **Couples, Adults** and **Teens:** All would appreciate the snow-cone/ ice cream gift card. In honor of Mr. Snowman's nose, carrot cake, cupcakes or muffins would be a great treat. There are beautiful snow globes that make wonderful keepsake gifts.
- For **Kids:** For those that do live in colder areas, igloo building molds would be a fun gift. A snow-cone making kit would be a big hit as well as a snow globe kit.

The Tenth Day of Christmas: January 3rd

What is SILVER at Christmas?...bells- jingle bells! Ice skates are also silver. Whether you are dashing through the snow or making perfect figure eights, being outside in the snow can get chilly. Give gifts to keep everyone warm.

Gift Ideas: (mix & match, pick & choose)

- For **Families**: Give a gift certificate to the local ice rink for a day of family fun. If they live in a warm climate, wind chime bells can be enjoyed all year long.
- For **Couples & Adults**: Hats, gloves, scarves or coats make great gifts. A light coat or sweatshirt works for those in warmer places. Hot tea and coffee baskets are great no matter where you live. Add some scones to round things out. For those that ski, snow-board, or go ice-fishing, give a gift card to the local sports store.
- For **Teens**: Along with the above ideas, hand and feet warmers are often over-looked but greatly appreciated when needed! And every teen I know loves to curl up with a warm blanket. For the readers, give the classic, "Hans Brinker and the Silver Skates" by Mary Maples Dodge.
- For **Kids**: Give hats, mittens, and/or ear warmers. Or give them a jingle bell bracelet to play along with their favorite carols.

The Eleventh Day of Christmas: January 4th

BROWN is today's color. We think of gingerbread, of course! We also think of the bare trees that have lost their leaves. Let's see if we can come up with some fun gifts made of wood.

Gift Ideas: (mix & match, pick & choose)
- For **Families & Couples:** There are some interesting personalized wooden gifts if you look online. Especially nice are the family plaques. Wooden board games or puzzles are a nice gift for all to enjoy. Wooden chopsticks would be fun. Or, make gingerbread treats for everyone!
- For **Couples & Adults:** They might like a wooden change dish or wood coasters. Wooden chopsticks are fun and you can include a gift card to a favorite Asian restaurant. If someone is a wood-worker, a gift card to the local hardware store would be much appreciated.
- For **Teens:** Teens might like the chopsticks. Wooden board games would be a hit. For the craft enthusiast, a wood-burning set might be just the thing.
- For **Kids:** Children would like wooden games and puzzles. There are interesting craft kits with wood available at local hobby shops. Of course, a gingerbread house kit would be great.

The Twelfth Day of Christmas: January 5th

This is the last day of your Christmas gift. I'm sure your giftees have really loved opening something unique each day. We will end with the color PURPLE. This is the color of royalty and we once again think of the wise men that brought their kingly gifts. Your gift for this day will recall that idea of luxury.

Gift Ideas: (mix & match, pick & choose)

- For **Families, Couples, Teens and Kids:** Think of a decadent dessert that would be enjoyed by all. Make it if you have a signature specialty. Or give a gift card to a restaurant known for their sweets. Very good caramel, butterscotch or hot chocolate sauce would be well received. It doesn't have to be a food item. Anything that they would not buy themselves (big or small) would be an item of luxury.
- For **Adults:** Specialty soaps or lotions would work here- they could treat their skin royally!
- For **Teens**: A fluffy, soft pillow is a treat. Or indulge their feet with cozy slippers or moccasins.
- For **Kids:** Children don't quite understand the luxury concept, but they will understand fun desserts and sauces!

Finishing Touches: Gift Tags

For your gift tags, print off the following. Glossy brochure paper works well. Print out the words as well on either the same paper or simply use copy paper. Cut out the tags, fold the first one in half. Cut out the word squares and glue or tape them inside or on the back of the corresponding tag. Don't forget to add your personal note! That is all you need to do. However, you can decorate the gift with picks, colored paper, or other embellishments. I gave a few examples of fun things to do with the tags throughout the book. I hope you have fun with them!

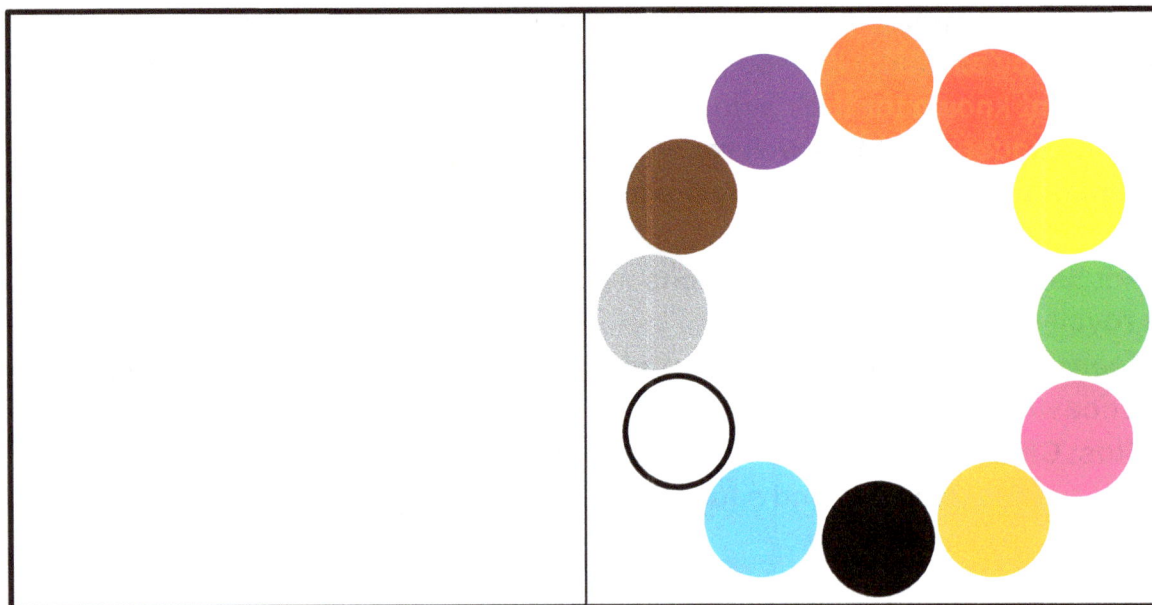

Inside Words:

You can simply write these words (or use your own- or both, if a short explanation is needed) inside the corresponding tag above, or you can make copies, cut them out and tape or glue them inside the gift tags

---

Merry Christmas!

Your gift this year is
12 Days of Christmas Color!
Each day's gift will focus on a different color and how that relates to Christmas.

CHEERS!

December 25th
The First Day of Christmas

ORANGE is the first day's color. This gift is inspired by a cozy fire in a stocking adorned fireplace.

December 26th
The Second Day of Christmas

The classic Christmas color is RED. Anything red is Christmassy!

December 27th
The Third Day of Christmas

YELLOW is the color of the day. What is yellow at Christmastime? The Bethlehem Star that the wise men followed! Today's gift revolves around the stars.

December 28th
The Fourth Day of Christmas

Today's color is another classic, GREEN! We see this color especially in wreaths, in decorating and, of course, the Christmas tree!

December 29th
The Fifth Day of Christmas

Today's color is PINK. Certainly not a traditional holiday color. What is pink? Why the Sugar Plum Fairy from the Nutcracker story!

December 30th
The Sixth Day of Christmas

Today's color is GOLD. At this time of year, we think of friends, both new and old. Remember the song phrase, "One is silver and the other gold?" Remember your gold friends today.

December 31st
The Seventh Day of Christmas

As the clock strikes midnight, the sky is BLACK- which is the color of seventh day of Christmas.

January 1st
The Eighth Day of Christmas

Today's color is BLUE. A blue winter sky is particularly beautiful in the morning. On this first morning of the new year, enjoy some "blue" inspired morning treats.

January 2nd
The Ninth Day of Christmas

WHITE is for...snow! This day's gifts will center around the cold fluffy stuff.

January 3rd
The Tenth Day of Christmas

What is SILVER at Christmas?...bells- jingle bells! Ice skates are also silver. Whether you are dashing through the snow or making perfect figure eights, enjoy the beauty and sounds of silver this season.

January 4th
The Eleventh Day of Christmas

BROWN is today's color. We think of gingerbread, of course! We also think of the bare trees that have lost their leaves, particularly pretty silhouetted against the evening sky.

January 5th
The Twelfth Day of Christmas

This is the last day of your Christmas gift. We will end with the color PURPLE. This is the color of royalty and once again we think of the wise men that brought their kingly gifts. Your gift for this day will recall that idea of luxury.

I hope you have as much fun putting these gifts together as I do! I know your recipients are going to love them. Now relax, have a glass of eggnog and enjoy the holidays. Cheers!

About the Author:

Christine Berg loves all things Christmas: the food, the traditions, the decorations. However, her favorite part is the gathering of family and friends, especially the ever-expanding families of her four adult children. She and her husband enjoy hosting in their Colorado home and cherish multi-generations and people of various cultural backgrounds laughing and celebrating together. All things Christmas can be a lot of work, though, and this book hopes to ease the burden. Visit her website for other books in this series: 12daystotherescue.com.

www.ingramcontent.com/pod-product-compliance
Lightning Source LLC
Chambersburg PA
CBHW080632030426
42336CB00018B/3162